Based on the philosophy of Charles C. Fries

Authors

Phyllis Bertin
Educational Coordinator
Windward School
White Plains, New York

Dr. Cecil D. Mercer
Professor of Education
University of Florida
Gainesville, Florida

Eileen Perlman
Learning Disabilities Specialist
White Plains Public Schools
White Plains, New York

Mildred K. Rudolph
Rosemary G. Wilson

Columbus, Ohio

A Division of The McGraw·Hill Companies

TABLE OF CONTENTS

Jane Banks	6
A Good Beginning	8
This House	10
Little Sam	12
Tammy	15
Freddy the Frog	18
Dr. Hunter's Tricks	21
The Book Clinic	24
A Sock Puppet	28
Something Different	30
Our Helpers	34
A Day With Dr. Hunter	36
A Sunday Picnic	38
At the Zoo	42
Back at School	45
Snakes at School	48
Who Am I?	52
Jane and the Rose Plant	54
A Rose	58
Spelling Jokes	60
Eggs for a Cake	61
Hank's List	64

SRA/McGraw-Hill

A Division of The McGraw·Hill Companies

Copyright © 1999 by SRA/McGraw-Hill. All rights reserved. Except as permitted under the United States Copyright Act, no part of this publication may be reproduced or distributed in any form or by any means, or stored in a database or retrieval system, without prior written permission from the publisher.

Printed in the United States of America.

Send all inquiries to:
SRA/McGraw-Hill
8787 Orion Place
Columbus, OH 43240

ISBN 0-02-674712-X

6 7 8 9 RRC 07 06 05

Let's Go to the Fair!	66
The Girl Who Kept Sheep	72
A Mixed-up, Very Bad Day	76
The Children's Band	78
The Deep Sea	84
A Trip to the Sea	90
A Man Named Red	96
Supper at the Lake	102
Red's Song	106
A Bike Race	108
Lunch at a Diner	114
At the Races	117
A Way To Make Money	120
The Zoo	126
A Map of the Zoo	129
To the Zoo	130
One Inch Taller	132
To the Teacher	137

cape

tape

cane

Jane

(which)   (across)

| tap | cap | can | cane |
| tape | cape | cane | Jane |

Jane Banks

One day Tam and Ted were on the way to school. Ted cannot see, so he had a cane to help him as he went along.

"Another girl will be in our class beginning today," said Tam. "Ms. King said something about her to Dan's mom. She's from another school."

"Which school did she go to?" asked Ted.

"I think she went to Franklin School," Tam said.

Ted tapped his cane as they went along. Tap, tap, tap. "Who is she?" he asked.

"Jane Banks," said Tam. "That's what Dan's mom said. Ted, that cane helps you a lot. How long have you had it?"

"Oh," said Ted, "I've had it a long time. I couldn't get along this well if I didn't have this cane."

When they got to school, they went up the steps into Ms. King's room. Tam went across the room, took off her cape, and hung it in the back of the room. Ted hung his jacket on a hook next to her cape. Just then a girl ran across the room. She ran into Tam, and Tam fell.

"Oh, my," said the girl, "let me help you up. I'm Jane Banks. I'm going to be in this class, but I think I'm off to a bad beginning."

"Well, let's just pretend we can go back and begin from here!" said Tam.

A Good Beginning

When Jane got home that day, her mother and father were there. "Well, tell us about your school and your class," said Mr. Banks.

"I got off to a bad beginning, but I think I'll like it. I was rushing across the room so I could hang my jacket before the bell rang. I bumped into a girl, and she fell, but she's OK. I like her, and I think I'll like the other kids," said Jane.

"How about Ms. King? Do you like her?" asked Mrs. Banks.

"Oh, yes," said Jane. "She's lots of fun. She said I'll have to get some tablets and some tape for spelling and math."

"Well, let's go to get your things now," said

Mrs. Banks. "Mrs. Benton's shop is still open, isn't it?"

"I think so," said Jane. "She can tell us which tablets are best. Her twins go to my school, but they aren't in my class. I think I've told you everything about my school. Do you think you will like your jobs?"

"I think I will," said Mr. Banks. "I have a good boss. She will be a big help."

"And I think my job will be a good one," said Mrs. Banks. "So we have a good house, a good school, and good jobs! I think we will be happy here!"

This House

Now this house has steps,
And that one did not.
Where that house had grass,
This has flowers in pots.

This one has a doghouse.
Our dog is so glad.
It's much better for her
Than that thin little pad.

This house may not be
Like the one from before,
But we're all happy here,
And we like it lots more!

ate

came

same

tame

name

game

son

at	Sam	same	game
ate	same	tame	name
		game	came

Little Sam

Little Sam was in Ms. Cook's room. He was in the same class as Pam. He ate in the lunchroom with the other boys and girls. He had the same books they had, and he played the same games. But it was a funny thing—Little Sam was not happy in school and he was not happy at home.

His mom got him a tame little black puppy for a pet, but that didn't help. The puppy jumped and jumped and licked Little Sam. But Sam was still sad.

Sam's dad took him camping in the woods. They looked for animals. They slept in a tent. Sam had fun. But still he looked sad.

At last Sam's mother took her son to the

doctor. Dr. Hunter looked at Sam for a long time. Then he said, "Little Sam is well, but I don't think he's happy."

Sam began to cry. "I don't like the name Little Sam!" he said. "I don't want to be little! I'm going to be little forever!"

"Oh, no, son," said his mom, "you are getting bigger every day!"

"No, I'm not," said Little Sam. "When I was six, I ran under a ladder. The man on the ladder sang a song to me:
'Under my ladder you ran, my lad.
You never will be as big as your dad!'"

Then Sam went on, "Well, that was a long time ago, and I look the same. I didn't get bigger!"

Dr. Hunter held his stick next to Sam and

said, "Stand still." Then he looked into his book. "Well, you did get bigger—seven inches bigger."

Next Dr. Hunter took his tape to see how long Sam's legs were. He checked the boy's hands and his fingers. He took a big book from a shelf to check something.

Then the doctor looked up from the book and said, "Sam, you can forget that man and his song. You will get to be as big as your dad, or bigger. You will not have the name Little Sam for long."

That made Sam very happy.

Tammy

Pam's dad took Kim and Pam to visit Jack and Pat Speck. They were thinking they would get to see the Specks' deer.

The Specks were glad to see them. "We're glad you came," said Pat. "You're just in time to see Tammy."

"Who is Tammy?" Kim and Pam asked.

"That's the name of our deer," said Pat. "We wanted her to have a name. So now she's Tammy."

"Do you see her a lot now?" Kim asked.

"We began playing this game, and now we see her every day," said Jack.

"Well, it isn't a game for Tammy," said Pat. "She just thinks she's getting fed."

Pam and Kim didn't understand.

"You see," Jack Speck went on, "one day we left some fresh grass, tender twigs, and some mushrooms on that big rock by the woods. Then when we came into the house, Tammy came from the woods. She ate everything we left for her. Now every day at the same time, we set something on the rock. And every day at the same time, she comes for dinner."

"So is she tame now?" Dad asked.

"She's as tame as she'll get, I think," said Jack. "She still won't come from the woods until we come into the house. And if we try to go up to her, she runs away."

Just then Pat said, "It's about that time. I'll take something to her rock. Look from this window. You'll get to see her."

"I like this game," said Pam. "Tammy gets fed, and we get to see her at last!"

hide

ride

side

ripe

pipe

hid	rid	rip	ripe
hide	ride	ripe	pipe
	side		

Freddy the Frog

"OK," said Ms. Cook, looking at the clock, "it's time to pass in your tests."

As the class was passing the tests in, Sam said to Pam, "That math test wasn't so bad."

"No," said Pam, "I'm glad we spent time the other day until we understood how to do it."

"Yes," Sam said, "that was a big help!"

Then Ms. Cook said, "We still have a little time. If you like, I can tell you a story before lunch."

"Oh, good!" said Pam and some others.

Ms. Cook took a book from the shelf and opened it. "This is the story of Freddy the frog," she began.

Freddy was a little frog. He played in the muddy spot by the side of the pond. One day he went swimming in the pond. He hopped from a pipe to a log that drifted by, and he took a long ride.

This was fun for Freddy. He said to himself, "My mother wants me to go to frog school, but I want to play in the pond."

Just then, Mother Frog came swimming along. "I'll hide from her," Freddy said. He liked to play tricks on his mother. So Freddy hid in the log. But what was inside the log with him? It was a long, funny-looking thing. It began to wiggle. Freddy began to giggle. "That's a funny-looking thing," Freddy said to himself. "Will it want to play?"

That funny-looking thing was a snake. Snakes like frogs, but not to play with. It jumped! Freddy hopped back just in time.

Freddy forgot the trick he was playing on his mother. He hopped to her side and said, "May I play with that long thing in the log? It can wiggle, and it can jump. It's funny!"

"Freddy!" Mother Frog said. "That's a snake! You must never play with snakes! You will have to go to frog school, my son. They will tell you at school not to play with things that wiggle. They will tell you lots of things that will help you."

"Yes, Mother, I'll go to frog school," Freddy said. "I'll be happy with the rest of the little frogs. I'll play in the muddy spot, and I'll swim in the pond, and I'll ride my log. But I'll never, ever play with things that wiggle!"

Ms. Cook's class clapped for the story, and then it was time for lunch.

Dr. Hunter's Tricks

When Dr. Hunter came to visit the sick children at the hospital, he did tricks for them. One day he said, "I have some metal clips in this hand. And here is a magnet. I'll do a trick with them. If you look, you can see that the clips will stick to the magnet."

He took a letter from his pocket. Then he shook the clips on top of the letter. He held the magnet next to the underside of the letter. The clips stood up on end. It looked just as if they wanted to get to the magnet!

Then Dr. Hunter said, "This time, I'll flip the letter so the magnet will be on top. The metal clips will not let go. They will stick to the letter."

Dr. Hunter flipped the letter so the magnet was on top. Not one clip fell from the bottom side of the letter. The magnet held the clips to the letter. It did not let them go.

Then the doctor said, "Next, I'll hide a clip under Ed's bed. The magnet will look for it. The clip can't hide from the magnet."

And it was just as Dr. Hunter said. He hid the clip under Ed's bed. Then he held the magnet under the bed. The clip slid to the magnet and stuck to it. Dr. Hunter held up the magnet, but the clip still hung on.

When Ed went back to school, he did some tricks with magnets for the class. The class asked him things like this.

> Can a magnet pick up a tin can?
> Can it stick to pipes?
> Can it pick up a ripe plum?

pale

paste

taste

waste

gave

brave

past	paste	pal	game
paste	waste	pale	gave
		paste	brave

The Book Clinic

Sam was trying to get to Ms. Long's room when he bumped into Mr. Mills.

"See what can happen when you run," said Mr. Mills. "Now, what is the big rush?"

"I'm going to Ms. Long's class," said Sam, "to help with the book clinic."

"Well, I don't blame you for rushing," Mr. Mills said. "But you shouldn't be running."

"Yes, Mr. Mills," said Sam as he took off.

When he got to Ms. Long's room, kids from every grade were there. Ms. Long was getting stuff from the cabinets. Some kids were standing by her desk. Kim and Jane were stacking books.

"The books in this stack are the ones we have to mend," said Jane.

Ms. Long began mixing paste in the mixer. "I'll have to mix a lot of paste then," she said.

After she had mixed the paste, they all began mending books. Some books had to be fixed with paste. Some had to be stitched along the sides. By the end of the day, they had fixed a lot of books.

"Not one book or a bit of paste went to waste today," said Jan.

"No," said Ms. Long, helping to stack books into boxes. "You all did a good job. The children at the hospital will be happy to get the books we fixed for them."

The next day a bus took Ms. Long and the others to the hospital. In one room a brave but pale little girl was getting a shot. "Well," Sam said to her, "you were very brave getting that shot. You didn't flinch at all."

The little girl grinned. Sam gave her a book. "This book is about a brave girl just like you," Sam said. "I think you'll like it."

In another room, Ted was telling a story to a little boy who had a bad cut on his leg. Another boy was in the room. He was very pale. He had a big pad and tape on his nose. Dan sat next to him.

"Pick the book you want," said Dan.

The boy picked a book about ships. "You have good taste in books," said Dan. "That's a very good book you picked."

"Thank you," the boy said.

Jan went into a room where a girl was dressed and sitting on the side of the bed.

"I had a bad rash, but I'm OK now. I'm going home today," said the girl.

"Well," said Jan, "how about a book to take home with you?"

All day Ms. Long and the boys and girls went from room to room. At last there were no books left.

Ms. Long told the children, "You did another very fine job. You gave away a lot of books, and you made some sick children very happy."

"Yes," said Sam, "what we did today felt so good!"

A Sock Puppet

Get this:

    A sock   A rubber band

    Some rags   Paste

    A stick

Do this:

1. Stuff the sock with rags.

2. Stuff one end of the stick into the sock.

3. Twist the rubber band onto the stick so the stick will stay in the sock.

4. Cut and paste a 😊 on your puppet.

slide

stripe

quite

life

wife

bit	rip	slid	wife
quit	strip	slide	life
quite	stripe		

Something Different

Dan, Jan, Jim, and Kim were on the way home from school one day. "We have quite a bit of time before supper," said Jan. "Let's do something different today, unless you have things to do for school."

"I don't," said Dan.

"I have math, but I can do it after supper," said Kim.

"What would you like to do?" asked Dan.

"Let's just think a second," said Jim. "We'll come up with something."

"How about a game of catch in the lot by Pam's house?" asked Kim.

"Fine!" said Jim, Jan, and Dan as they began to run to the lot. They were all happy as they ran along. But things were quite different when they got to the lot. There were torn sacks, old lunches, and bits of glass dumped on the lot. They all stopped running and just looked at it.

"What a mess!" said Jim. "Well, if we want to play catch here, we'll have to pick up this junk."

"I'll grant you that," said Dan. "Let's dig in."

They began to pick up the trash and drop it into the trash cans by the side of the lot. It didn't take them long to get things picked up. Jan picked up the last bit of glass and took it to the trash can. Just as she got there, she slipped, and the glass began to slide from her hand.

"Oh, no!" she said. "I've cut myself!"

"Let me look at it," said Jim. "Yes, that's

quite a cut. I'll run to Pam's house and get Mr. Sands. You just sit here."

Jim was back in no time with Pam and Mr. Sands. Jan's cut had bled quite a lot by then. "Well, kids," said Mr. Sands, "I think we'd better take a little trip to the hospital. Jan just may get a stitch in that cut."

Jan grinned at Dan, trying to look brave. "Why don't you run home and tell Mom and Dad?" she said.

"OK," said Dan. "We'll be at the hospital as fast as we can."

Dan and Mr. Bell got to the hospital just seconds after Mr. Sands, Jan, and the others. A doctor took Jan into a little room with stripes on the walls. Mr. Bell said, "I must try to get my wife. I'll be back in a second."

When Mr. Bell got back, he said, "She's on her way." Then they all just sat on the hospital bench, looking at the stripes on the walls.

It wasn't long before Mrs. Bell came in looking for her husband. She rushed up to him just as the doctor and Jan came back.

"We're all going to miss our suppers," Jan said with a grin. She held up the hand with the cut. It had a big dressing on it. Jan looked at the dressing and said, "Well, that's life! I said I wanted to do something different today, and I did!"

Our Helpers

1. You may catch a bus here.

2. This tells you, "Do not go in this way."

3. This tells you, "You may ride your bike here."

4. This tells you, "Do not drop trash here."

hope   joke

              broke

note   broken

rode   bone

              alone

drove

(their)

not	hop	rod	joke
note	hope	rode	broke
		drove	broken

A Day With Dr. Hunter

Dr. Hunter was alone in a cab. He was on his way to the hospital. As he rode along, he made a note of some things he had to do. "I must stop by and see the woman in Room 105 who broke her leg. I can do that after I go to the clinic," he said to himself. "Then I can visit the sick boys and girls." He liked to visit the sick children. He would do tricks and tell them jokes, and sometimes they felt better.

At the clinic, Dr. Hunter stopped to see Frank and Fred Hicks. They had infected tonsils. When Dr. Hunter came in, Mr. and Mrs. Hicks were sitting on the clinic bench with their sons. Fred looked at Dr. Hunter and began to slide along the bench. At last he was sitting at the very end.

"Come back here and sit next to us," said

his mother. "The doctor will look at you next."

Dr. Hunter took a magnet from his pocket. He began to do tricks for Frank. Fred slid back to look at the tricks.

Dr. Hunter looked at the boys' tonsils. Then he said, "Have the boys take the pills in this box for ten days, one pill a day. Then bring them back for a checkup."

"I hope they will not have to miss much school," said Mr. Hicks.

"Oh, just a day or so," said Dr. Hunter. "Good-by now. Take your pills, and don't forget your checkups." Then Mr. and Mrs. Hicks drove their sons home.

Next Dr. Hunter visited the woman with the broken bone. After that he did what he liked best. He visited the sick children.

A Sunday Picnic

One day Dan and Jan's dad said to the family, "Why don't we have a picnic today? It's such a sunny day!"

Mom said, "I'd like that. We can pack a basket and go to that spot by the pond where we camped last summer."

They went into the kitchen. Mom began to hand things to Dan and Jan. She gave them hot dogs, plastic bags filled with buns, and bananas. Then she gave them packets of ketchup and mustard.

Dan asked, "Mom, why don't we take the other ketchup?"

"I don't want to risk broken glass," said Mom.

Just then Dad came in with a chest filled with cold drinks. Dan took the basket, and

Jan took the chest of cold drinks. They set them in the van.

Then they ran back into the kitchen. "I think we have everything," said Dan. "May we take Nat and Rags? I don't like for them to be alone."

"Not today," said Mom. "It's very hot for Nat and Rags. It's better for them at home."

Then they all got into the van.

As Dad drove along, he and Mom told some funny things that had happened to them. Then they told jokes and sang songs. The jokes and the songs made the long ride fun.

Then Dad said, "Well, here we are!" He backed the van into a good spot next to a grill and a picnic bench.

Dan asked, "Should I look for some wood so we can cook the hot dogs?"

"Not today, Dan," said Mom. "Just get that bag from the back of the van."

Dan looked into the van. "Do you want this black, lumpy stuff?" he asked.

"That's it," said Mom.

Dan cooked the hot dogs in just a short time. Mom, Dad, and Jan had to rush to set up the rest of the things.

They all liked this picnic spot. "This is just fine," said Dad. "There are no chicken bones, torn napkins, or broken glass here. When we finish, we must dump our trash into the trash cans. Then the next family to picnic here will have a good spot for their lunch."

use

cute

cube

tube

tune

zoo

us	cub	tub	tube
use	cube	tube	cube
		tune	cute

At the Zoo

Ms. King, Ms. Cook, and Mr. Mills all wanted to take their classes to the zoo. They planned to use the same bus. When the day came for the zoo trip, everyone felt quite happy. They sang tunes along the way.

The woman at the gate of the zoo asked everyone to get in line to pay. But Ms. Cook said, "I have the money for everyone. We collected it at school."

Just inside the gate was a pen with an ostrich in it. The ostrich had a long neck and long legs. Kim looked and looked at the ostrich. When they got to the pond, she said, "Oh, look at that little pink ostrich!"

Mr. Mills said, "It looks a little like an ostrich, Kim, but it's a flamingo!"

Everyone stayed at the pond a long time. They wanted to see the otters playing. The otters slid on a long mud slide and splashed into the pond. It looked like fun.

Next everyone went to visit the snakes. "They look like long tubes to me," said Jim.

Then the classes looked at tanks and tanks of fish—black fish, gray fish, fish with red fins, and fish with stripes.

Mr. Mills wanted to save the visit to the ape pens till the end. When they got to them at last, the children liked the cute little ape best of all.

Pam said, "It looks so tame. I would like to have it for a pet."

Then Ms. King asked Pam, "But do you think it will be tame when it gets big?"

"No," said Pam, "it won't be tame, and it

will be very strong. Maybe I wouldn't want it for a pet after all."

"Well," said Dan, "I still think it's cute."

The little ape looked up at Dan. Then it picked up a nut and held it up to him. "And it thinks you're cute, Dan!" Pam said with a giggle.

At last the children sat on some benches to have lunch and rest. Ms. Cook gave them all cold drinks with lots of cubes in them. The drinks tasted quite good after such a long morning.

In the bus on the way back to school, the classes asked riddles to pass the time. Here are some of them.

"I am very long and look like a tube. I wiggle when I go from spot to spot. Who am I?"

"I picked up a nut and wanted Dan to have it. Who am I?"

Back at School

It was late when everyone got back from the zoo. Mr. Mills said to his class, "We won't have time to do much math or spelling. What would you like to do with the rest of our day?"

Some of the boys and girls wanted to play games. But Mr. Mills said, "You can play games after school. We should think of a better way to use our school time."

Jim said, "We could sing a tune. Maybe we could make up a song about the apes or the ostriches at the zoo."

Jan said, "That's a good way to use the time. Maybe we could look at some books about the animals at the zoo. Ms. Cook has some good books about animals in her room."

Frank said, "Maybe we could use her books.

Then later some of us could make up a story about an animal. We could make up a class book about animals."

Jim said, "I'll make up some tunes for the book. Then we can have a sing-along!"

Jan said, "I'll see if Ms. Cook will let us use some of her books."

Frank and some of the others got together and began to make up a story.

When the bell rang, Mr. Mills said, "I think all of you used your time quite well. We can finish this class book in the morning. This was a good day for all of us."

bake

lake

Jake

safe

five

live

drive

alive

back	Jack	like	live
bake	Jake	life	five
lake	take	live	drive

Snakes at School

After the class trip to the zoo, Ms. King began to plan lessons on snakes. She sent a letter to the zoo asking for help.

A letter came back from Miss Betty Jones. It was her job to look after the live snakes at the zoo. In the letter Miss Jones said, "We have five snakes that we take to schools. I like to bring them myself. If I have them along with me, it will help your class get a better understanding of snakes."

The next day Betty slid the boxes of snakes onto some racks in the zoo truck. Jake Hill went along to help.

It was hot as they drove along. Jake said, "Your snakes don't have much room in their boxes. They'll bake in there. Let's drive by the lake so the truck will be in the shade."

So they did. Then Betty said, "I want to stop and check things in the back of the truck. Why don't you have your lunch? I'll take a look at the snakes."

Jake sat in the grass and ate his lunch. Betty went to look into the back of the truck. The box with the blacksnake had shifted onto its side. The snake wiggled from the box and slid from the truck.

"Get that snake!" yelled Betty. Then she shut the truck.

Jake dropped his lunch and ran to a man who was cutting grass. "Let me use your rake," he said. "I have to pick up a live snake that belongs to the zoo. If I don't, it will get away. It's very fast!"

Jake lifted the snake with the rake. Then he rushed back to Betty, who held the snake's box in her hands. When the snake was safe in the box, Jake got very pale. He sat on the grass and said to Betty, "I'll never be brave with live snakes!"

But Betty said, "You don't have to be brave to handle live snakes. You just have to understand the best things to do. I am glad you used a rake and didn't try to pick up the snake with your hands. But you were safe just the same. The snakes we take to schools don't have fangs that can kill."

Jake was glad of that. He felt better.

After Betty spoke to the class, the children clapped for her. She gave Ms. King this list of nine things to tack up:

1. Snakes can be big or little.
2. Snakes can go very fast.
3. Snakes can be helpful. They can get rid of insects and pests.

4. A snake can lunch on something that is bigger than itself.
5. Some very big snakes can crush a person.
6. Blacksnakes are hatched from eggs.
7. Little rattlesnakes are born alive and wiggling.
8. A snake has no legs, but it has a long backbone and lots of ribs.
9. A snake's skin can help it hide. Thin snakes look like twigs when they are still. Thick snakes can look like logs.

Then Betty said to the class, "If you get a book on snakes, it will tell you lots of things I didn't have time for."

Ms. King said, "I'm glad you said that, Miss Jones. Class, here on this bookshelf are books on snakes. Thank you, Miss Jones, for a fine lesson."

Who Am I?

| Metal | Glass | Brick |
| Wood | Rubber | Plastic |

1. I may shatter when you drop me.

2. I will sink in a lake.

3. I will jump back up when you drop me.

4. I shine, but I may rust.

5. I can bend.

Can you think of some things that are made of metal, glass, brick, rubber, plastic, or wood?

hose

rose

those

these

note	rose	hose	those
nose	hose	rose	these
		those	

Jane and the Rose Plant

Mother's Day was just five days away. Jane Banks wanted to get her mother a gift. Her mother had an interest in plants. So Jane asked Tam to help her pick a gift for her mother.

"Your mother has an interest in plants," Tam said. "Why not get her a plant?"

"I was thinking of a plant," Jane told Tam. "Yes, that will be good. Do you think you could go to Peg's Plant Shop with me after school? We could pick a plant today, and I'll ask Peg to let me pick it up the day before Mother's Day."

"Yes, I'd like to go with you," said Tam. "I always like going to Peg's. It's such fun to look at all those plants. I think I like the roses best."

"Well, how about today after school?" asked

Jane. "Do you have things you have to do?"

"No, today is fine with me," said Tam, "as long as I'm home in time for supper."

When they got to Peg's later that day, Jane looked at some plants with red roses on them. "One of these would be fine, don't you think?" asked Jane.

Tam was looking at a man spraying red roses with a long hose. She looked at Jane and said, "Oh, I think that one is fine. Maybe by Mother's Day some of the buds will be open. Oh, look at these, Jane! Do you like these pink roses?"

"I like these red roses, but I think I like those pink ones better," said Jane. "The buds should be open by Mother's Day, and they will smell so good!"

"Well, let's look at all of them and select the best rose plant in the shop," said Tam.

"Do you think my mom will like this?" asked Jane as she picked up one plant.

"That one has thorns!" said Tam.

"Why do some roses have thorns?" Jane asked.

"To protect them, silly!" said Tam. "That's their way of stopping you from cutting or picking them."

"And it's a good way, isn't it?" said Jane.

When Jane had picked the rose plant she wanted, she took it to Peg. "You picked a fine plant," said Peg as she held a rose to her nose to sniff it. "You can pick it up the day before Mother's Day. I'll set it in the back room until then. And I'll spray it with a hose every day so it will stay fresh. Those buds should be open on Mother's Day. It will be a fine gift."

"Thanks a lot," said Jane. "I hope my mom likes it."

"Oh, she will," said Peg. "Roses make a very good gift for Mother's Day."

A Rose

One morning as I went along
A path that I did see,
I came upon a little rose
As red as red could be.

I stopped to look upon the rose
That popped up in my way.
I bent to pick it—but I stopped,
And went my happy way.

That rose was not for me alone;
A rose can never be.
Let others look upon that rose,
And all its glory see.

sail

tail

pail

mail

Gail

waist

pale	sale	pale	mail
sale	tale	pail	tail
	tail	mail	sail

Spelling Jokes

Ms. Cook's class made up jokes to fit a spelling list. Linda said this:

> I'll tell you a tale
> of a little pig's tail.
> It will be a long tale
> of a very short tail.

Sam made up this joke:

> When Jill dropped her pail,
> she looked quite pale.

His pal Sally said this:

> Let's sail this ship
> to the sale on sails.
> Will these sails on sale
> help the ship to sail?

Pam said this:

> A man who won't let
> a bite go to waste
> will never get a belt
> to fit his waist.

Eggs for a Cake

One fine sunny morning, Gail's mother was going to her class. As she left, she said to Gail, "Here is some money. Could you go to Mrs. Benton's shop later? I want some eggs to bake a cake when I get home."

That made Gail very happy. She was going to be eleven today. Her mother didn't have to tell her the cake was for her.

Gail had to pass the mailbox on her way to school. She looked into the box. There were six letters, and five of them were for her! "I won't open them yet," she said. "I'll stop at Mrs. Benton's on my way home and get the eggs. Then we can all look at my letters before dinner."

Gail had a good day at school. All day she kept thinking about her mail and the cake her mom would bake for her. But thinking about it just made the day drag. At last, the school bell rang. Quick as a flash Gail was on her way to Mrs. Benton's shop.

Gail was going so fast she didn't see the little pail by Jill's desk. She hit her leg on it and had to catch herself. She set the pail back where it belonged and was on her way. "Not so fast," she said to herself.

Mrs. Benton was having a sale on eggs that day. Gail got plenty for a very big cake. She was humming as she left the shop. Just by the shop was a little dog. Gail was thinking about her cake and not about dogs' tails. All of a sudden, she fell—and there she was with broken eggs in her lap and a crying dog next to her!

Gail picked herself up and gave the dog a pat. Lots of the eggs had broken. "Oh, no," she said to herself. "I hope these will do for a cake."

When she got home, her mother was there. "What happened to you?" she asked Gail.

After Gail had told her about everything, Gail's mother said, "Well, don't be upset. Let's get a rag to wipe you off. Why don't you look at your mail, and I'll bake the cake. It may be a little cake, but there will be room for eleven candles."

Hank's List

Hank made a list of all the things he has to do today. Then he checked (✓) all the things he finished.

Here is Hank's list:
- ✓ 1. Cut the grass.
- ✓ 2. Go to the bank.
- ✓ 3. Mail the letter to Ms. Kelly.
-     4. Pay the gas bill.
- ✓ 5. Go to the plant shop.
-     6. Mend my black slacks.

Did Hank mail a letter?

Did he finish all the things on his list?

Tell what things Hank still has to do.

Make a list of things you want to do after school today.

Check the things you finish.

paid

laid

rain

pain

paint

plain

fair

pair

hair

wait

pain	made	cane	pain
pair	paid	plane	pair
paid	laid	plain	fair

Let's Go to the Fair!

Gail came home from school the next day with a note. This is what it said:

Mothers and Fathers,

Our school always takes some time off when the fair begins. So beginning Monday the fifth, there will be no school for five days. We will use the time to paint the classrooms. School will open the next Monday.

Thank you,
Ms. Kent

At dinner Mrs. Bond said to her husband, "Gail will not have school when the fair begins. I think it would be a good time to take a little trip. I can get some time off from my job. Do you think you can?"

"Yes, I think so. That would be a good time to go to the state fair," said Mr. Bond.

"Fine," said Mrs. Bond. "Do you want to take a bus?"

"I think that would be quite a trip by bus. The bus ride is longer than you would think. An airplane ride would be fun, but we would have to pay quite a fare. Besides, we would have to take a cab to the airport. So I think we'd better take the bus," said Mr. Bond.

Mr. and Mrs. Bond were up at six the day they were going to the fair. They made the bed and then laid their bags on it. They packed a pair of big bags and one little bag.

Just after seven, Mrs. Bond woke Gail. Then they all went into the kitchen and ate. Gail said, "I'm going to have to rush to fix my hair."

"And bring your rain hat, the plain red one. If it rains, you will be glad to have it," said Mrs. Bond.

"OK, Mom," said Gail. "I'll be quick."

When she got back, Mr. and Mrs. Bond were waiting for her. "We're off!" said Mrs. Bond.

When they got to the bus terminal, Mrs. Bond said, "We're running late. We'll have to rush." So they grabbed their bags and ran all the way to the ticket desk.

There were seven sailors in line at the ticket desk. They were trying to get tickets so they could get back to their ship. That took a long time! The Bonds had to wait and wait. "We may miss our bus if we have to wait much longer," said Mr. Bond.

At last the sailors left, and Mr. Bond spoke to the ticket woman. "We would like tickets for the bus going to the state fair."

"Yes," said the woman, "here they are. Your bus will be at Gate Five."

Mrs. Bond said, "I can pay for them, Ken. I just got paid." So she took some money from her handbag and laid it on the ticket desk. Then the woman at the desk handed them their tickets and clipped red tags on the handles of their bags.

"I'm afraid we'll still have to rush," said Mr. Bond. "Let's go. We can just make it to Gate Five in time."

It was quite a long way from the ticket desk to Gate Five. The family rushed so much that Gail got a pain in her side from running.

"Oh, wait a second," she said. "I have to rest just a bit."

"We can't stop now!" said her mother. "I'll take your bag. Then you can go faster."

The Bonds got to Gate Five just in the nick of time! Gail's pain didn't last very long, but they were all huffing and puffing. They were on their way to the state fair!

feed   deep

need   keep

            sheep

meet   creep

feet   steep

feel

heel

fed	fell	met	deep
feed	feel	meet	steep
feet	heel	feet	sheep

The Girl Who Kept Sheep

Long ago there was a girl named Nan. One day she met a woman who had a big flock of sheep.

The woman said, "I must take a trip, and I'll need a girl with lots of pep to tend my sheep for a short time. Do you want the job, Nan?"

"Oh, yes," Nan told her, "I need a job."

"Good," said the woman. "I'll be home for the next five days. You can meet with me and take some sheep-tending lessons on those days. You will handle the sheep well after you have had lessons. I think you will do a good job."

"I hope I understand the lessons," Nan said to herself.

When the five days had passed, the woman

said good-by and wished Nan good luck. Then Nan went to tend the sheep. She drove the sheep to the spot with the best grass. The sheep began to feed on it. The woman had said, "Do not let the sheep get on the steep hill. If they get on the hill, they will slide into the pond. Use the big stick to keep them on the flat grass. If you can do that much, they will just creep along as they feed."

Nan kept looking at the sheep as they ate. Then she said, "My feet feel funny from standing so much. Do I have to stand to tend sheep? I bet I can sit and still do a good job." So she sat.

After a short time, Nan got up and went to a spot in the shade to sit. She fell into a deep sleep, and when she woke, she looked for the sheep.

"Good, they're still here," she said. "These sheep understand they mustn't slide into the pond. This job isn't quite so bad as I kept thinking."

The next day, Nan didn't stand to look at her flock. She sat. Then she went to sleep with the stick still in her hand. The stick dropped. Bang! It fell and struck a rock. Nan woke up! She looked for her flock. No sheep!

She ran to the steep hill. No sheep! She looked into the pond. No sheep! Nan ran from spot to spot. She looked this way and that. She got as red as a beet, but still, no sheep! At last she went deep into the woods. There was her flock, nibbling grass along the path.

Nan used her stick to drive the sheep from the woods, tapping them on the sides to make them run. At last she collected them and drove them back to a safe spot.

The unhappy girl had a pain in her heel from a thorn. She was quite lame when she took a step, but she didn't sit this time.

"I can blame myself for this," Nan said. "It's not good to sleep and tend sheep at the same time. I'm lucky the sheep are still alive and that they didn't slide into the pond."

At last the woman came home. She was happy. "You did a fine job," she told Nan. "I think my lessons must have helped you."

"Yes, they helped," Nan was thinking, "but not as much as the lesson I had after you left. One must never sleep when tending sheep."

A Mixed-up, Very Bad Day

It was not a good day, not good at all.
Oh, things were very bad!
I'll tell you my story, and you will see
Just how bad a day I had.

I ran to the bus stop to catch a plane,
And the ship forgot its sail.
I went to the bank to cash a check,
And the dentist took my mail!

My cat was so sad she grinned all day,
And my dog got wet in the sun.
The rain fell up and bumped the sky,
And Peggy said, "This is fun!"

week   steer

seek   queer

peek

                        seem

sweet

street   seen

                        teens

tree

three

see	sleep	see	tree
tree	steep	seen	street
three	steer	seem	sweet

The Children's Band

Nell liked to do lots of things. She liked to fish at the lake and camp in the woods with her father. She liked to help in the kitchen. One time Nell fixed some punch all by herself, but it didn't taste sweet. It had a queer taste! It was so bitter it made her lips pucker, and that was funny!

Nell liked to play hide-and-seek with her little sister, Candy, but Candy liked to peek. So Nell tricked her and hid in a tree.

Nell liked to ride her bike. She could steer as well as her big sister, Fran. Fran was fifteen or sixteen. Nell forgot just how old Fran was, but she was in her teens. Sometimes Fran would take Nell and Candy to the zoo. That was lots of fun!

And sometimes Nell just liked to be alone.

Then she would sit under the big tree at the back of the house. That was her thinking spot.

Nell liked to do all these things, but best of all, she liked to play her drums. She would stick her drumsticks into her pocket so she could have them with her all the time. One day the Children's Band was asked to play on May Day.

"The Children's Band will play in three weeks," Nell told her father. "They will play on Main Street with all the big bands, and I want to play with them."

"Then you'll have to get in the band," her father said. "You're a good drummer."

Nell looked sad and said, "There are nineteen in the band. Three of them are drummers. I don't think they need me."

"If you ask, I bet they'll let you play," said her father. "You're a good drummer. Just ask them and see."

Nell nodded. "OK," she said at last. "I'll ask Deb and Bob and Ron. They're the drummers in the Children's Band. I hope they'll want me to play."

That Monday after school, Nell asked if she could play in the band on May Day.

"We have three drummers. We don't need another," said Deb. "Could you play a flute?"

"No, I can't play a flute," Nell said. "I'm a drummer—a good drummer—and I bet I can play as well as all of you!"

"Well, play by yourself," Bob said. "We don't need a drummer!"

When Nell got home, she was upset.

Fran said, "You seem so sad, Nell. What happened?"

Nell didn't feel like telling her. She had a queer feeling, and she wanted to be alone. She took her drumsticks from her pocket and sat under a tree. A bee began to buzz beside her nose. "Go away!" Nell said and hit at the bee. "I want to think." Then someone yelled from the street. It was Bob with Ron and Deb.

"What brings you here?" Nell said. She still seemed mad.

"We have something to tell you," said Ron.

"Well," Nell said, "OK." Then they all sat under the tree with Nell.

"The things we said to you today weren't fair," Ron said, "and we wish we had not said them."

Then Deb said, "We think you're a good drummer, and we want to make it up to you. We hope you will play in the band with us on May Day."

"Pals?" they asked.

Nell looked at Bob, and she looked at Ron and Deb. At last she said, "Pals!"

Nell led the band on May Day. She had never seen a better day. She played her drum better than ever. And all the children in the band clapped for her.

"Nell is the very best drummer!" they said.

"She's the best in the band!" said Deb, Ron, and Bob.

As for Nell, she was so happy she kept her May Day smile all that week.

meat   read
beat
eat   real
treat   heal

sea   dear
tea   hear

sea	meet	heel	dear
see	meat	heal	deer
seem	beat	real	steer

The Deep Sea

For a long time, Jim Benton had liked books about animals. He had five books about horses. He had lots of books about dogs and cats. After his visit with Pat and Jack Speck, Jim went to a bookshop and got a book about deer. "They are such dear little things," he said to himself. He really liked to sit with a cup of tea and read about animals.

One day Jim's grandpa gave him a book about the sea. "What a treat!" Jim said. "It looks like a neat book! I think I'll go read it now, if that's OK with you."

"Yes, that's fine with me," said Jim's grandpa. "I'm glad to hear you like it, Jim. It took me a long time to pick a good book for you."

Jim went into the kitchen and made

himself some tea. Then he took his teacup and his book into his bedroom. He sat on his bed and began to read about the sea. That was just the beginning.

From then on, Jim was always looking for books about the sea. He went to bookshop after bookshop looking for different books about the sea. He looked at every book about the sea his school had. Whenever Grandpa came visiting, Jim would say, "Tell me about the sea. I like to hear all about it. I can't see the sea from my house, but I can read about it. And I can hear about it. Tell me everything you can about the sea, Grandpa."

"That's a good hobby," said Grandpa. "Maybe someday you can go to sea. Do you think you'd like being a sailor?"

"That's not really what I want," said Jim. "I just want to understand all about fish and the plant life in the sea." Then Jim began to read books about fish. He got some books about shellfish—lobsters, crabs, and shrimp. Jim always seemed to have a book about shellfish with him.

He made a list of some things that were interesting to him.

1. Shellfish come from eggs and hatch in the sea.
2. Lobsters, crabs, and shrimp have feelers. These feelers may help them to smell.
3. Lobsters, crabs, and shrimp can see.
4. They can bite into things and eat.
5. They have feet that help them get from spot to spot.
6. Shellfish can heal themselves.
7. They do not have real skins, but they do have a sort of crust that is like a thin shell.

8. Lots of shops sell lobster, crab, and shrimp meat. Some say the taste of meat from shellfish can't be beat.

Next Jim looked for books about the plants of the sea, such as reeds and seaweed. At last he got a book on jellyfish and one on clams.

On his next visit Grandpa said, "I took a ride on a skiff with a glass bottom one time. I got to see lots of jellyfish and seaweed and lots of different fish that way. I really had a good time."

"Grandpa," said Jim, "will you take me with you if you go back? I want to see all those queer fish and the plants in the sea! I'll save my money for the plane fare if you will just take me! I'll save my money beginning with this dime!"

"Well, add this dime to that one and you are off to a good beginning. Let's make some plans now!" said Grandpa.

weak   leaf

beak

speak   least

            beast

peach   east

teach

each   cheap

does

leaf	beak	week	each
least	speak	weak	peach
beast	cheap	beak	teach

A Trip to the Sea

Jim began to save his money. He really wanted to go east on a deep-sea trip with Grandpa. But he still didn't have much in the bank when Grandpa wanted to go.

One day Grandpa and Grandma came to Jim's house for dinner. Jim was not at home. He was at a club meeting nearby where he was going to speak.

Grandpa said to Jim's mom and dad, "I'll be going on that deep-sea fishing trip in about a week. Does my grandson still want to go with me?"

"Oh, my, yes," said Jim's mom. "He has kept all his money for this trip. But he still doesn't have as much as he needs. He does lots of little jobs to get money, but it will take a long time for him to save the money."

"Well, it's just a shame," said Grandma. "I think it's just a shame Jim has to wait till he has the money. Just think of the plane fare for a trip like that! It would take him forever to save that much!"

Then Grandpa said, "I think the airlines have cheaper rates for boys and girls than they used to have. Let me check. It may be quite cheap."

Grandma said, "I can help with the fare, at least a little."

Mother said, "If it is cheaper, maybe we can scrape up the money."

"If Jim stays in my hotel room, that will save some money," said Grandpa. "If we each chip in, Jim can go on the trip."

Dad said, "Can you wait until the week after next? Jim is in school until then."

"Oh, I can wait," said Grandpa. "Now let me check on the plane fare."

When he got back, Grandpa said, "I took care of everything. We have to be at the airline desk by nine in the morning on Monday, June tenth."

Just then, Jim got back from his meeting. Grandpa said to him, "You'd better begin packing."

"Packing?" said Jim. "Why?"

"For your trip east to the sea," said Grandpa.

"Oh, wow!" said Jim.

So in the second week in June, Jim and his grandpa stepped onto a plane. They had a good plane ride. A van took them to the hotel. Jim quickly got into a pair of shorts and ran to the beach in his bare feet.

The next day Jim and his grandfather took a ride in a skiff with a glass bottom. Jim asked the skipper, "Does this thing leak? Is the glass bottom weak?"

"My skiff is not the least bit weak. It will be fine," the skipper told Jim.

Just then Grandpa yelled, "Jim, look!"

Jim yelled back, "Oh, wow! Look at the long tail on that fish! That one looks like a real beast."

Then the skipper said, "There is a jellyfish. Some say it looks like a bell or a leaf. In the sea, fish can look like plants, and plants can look like fish."

"I will ask my teacher to teach us about these fish," said Jim.

The skipper kept looking for fish. "Look at that one," she said. There was one that looked like a peach with a nose. Another looked like a snake. And another looked as if it had a big beak.

"What queer-looking fish!" Jim said.

When the sun began to set, the skipper said they had to get the skiff back. She liked Jim so much she gave him a pile of snapshots of different fish.

When Jim reached home, he fixed the snapshots on his dresser. He never wanted to forget his trip.

taping

baking

taking

making

shaking

hoping

using

tap	back	hope	taping
tapping	backing	hoping	taking
taping	baking	hopping	shaking

A Man Named Red

One day Dr. Santis was taking care of some sick boys and girls at the clinic. Dr. Hunter came up to her. "May I speak to you, Beth?" he said.

"I'll be with you in a second," she said. "Just let me finish taping this boy's leg. He fell and got quite a big gash." When she had finished taping the boy's leg, Dr. Santis went to Dr. Hunter.

"Now, Don," she said, "what can I do for you?"

"Beth," said Dr. Hunter, "I have taken care of a man for six weeks now. His leg was badly broken, but it is much better now. He is using a crutch and is doing quite well. He no longer needs to stay in the hospital."

"I'm glad he is doing well," said Dr. Santis. "But what has this got to do with me?"

"Well," said Dr. Hunter, "he needs a job. I was told that you and your husband were looking for someone to take care of your children."

"Yes," said Dr. Santis. "Lately we have had to take them to a sitter's house. I was hoping we would come across someone who could take care of them at our house."

"Well," said Dr. Hunter, "I'd like you to meet Red. He likes children. He has taken care of kids before. He has a letter from the last family he stayed with. He's a good man."

"Well, when can I meet him?" asked Dr. Santis.

"He's waiting in his room now."

"Well, let's go," said Dr. Santis.

As Red and Dr. Santis were shaking hands, they felt they would like each other. "I'd like to have you stay with us and take care of the children," said Dr. Santis. "Can you go home with me today? I'd like my husband, Dom, and the children to meet you before I offer you the job."

"That's just fine with me," said Red. "Dr. Hunter said I can go whenever I want."

"Good," said Dr. Santis. "I'll stop by for you later. Cross your fingers. But I think they will like you as much as I do."

Later that day, Beth Santis took Red to meet her family. They all liked Red and wanted him to stay with them. Red seemed to enjoy baking, making the beds, dusting, and cooking. The children really liked him. His crutch didn't keep him from playing games with them or doing lots of things. Red and the Santis family were quite happy.

One day Red said to Beth, "May I go to the clinic with you today? I am to see Dr. Hunter. I hope I can stop using this crutch. Wish me luck."

"Yes," said Dr. Santis. "I think Dom can stay with the children till you get back."

At the clinic, Dr. Hunter began to press on Red's leg with his fingers. He asked Red if his leg pained him. "Not much," said Red.

Then Dr. Hunter said, "Bend your leg for me. Good. You must try to bend and unbend your leg at least a hundred times each day. You can stop using your crutch and stop taping your leg. I am hoping your leg will get stronger with no crutch. Come back to see me in about six weeks."

Six weeks later Red's leg was so much better he could drive himself to the clinic. He came home grinning after that trip. "Dr. Hunter said my leg is all better. I won't be using a crutch. I can do whatever I wish," he said.

"I'm so glad," said Mr. Santis. "I hope you'll stay with us."

"I would be happy to stay," said Red. "Now I can take the children to the pond to swim. I can teach them to ride a horse. We can do a lot of things together."

"We will have lots of very happy days," said Dr. Santis. "I'm glad you came to stay with us."

hiking   diving

          driving

hiding

riding   biting

sliding

          poking

          joking

(too
  tooth)

hike	bite	joke	riding
hiking	biting	joking	sliding
hiding	hiding	poking	driving

Supper at the Lake

One hot day in June, Dom was driving past the lake. Red was with him. "Look at those boys and girls diving into the lake!" said Red. "It makes me feel like jumping in, too!"

"Well," said Dom, "let's get Beth and the kids and have supper here. We can pack a picnic basket quick as a wink. Last week, when we took the kids hiking, we had that lunch packed in no time! A day like today is made for picnics."

When they reached home, Red went looking for the children. He had quite a time with Kathy. She liked to play tricks on him by hiding in a different spot every day. This time she was hiding under the stairs.

They were glad to be going to the lake. Everyone helped pack the picnic lunch. Dom made sandwiches. Red helped by sliding each sandwich into a little plastic bag. Then he packed them in the picnic basket. Beth made a jug of punch and filled a second jug with milk. Manny took the basket and the plastic jugs to the truck. Then his mom gave him some bananas, peaches, and plums.

Red yelled for Kathy and Bill. They ran up and hopped into the truck with the rest of the family. In just a second they were riding along on their way to the lake.

At the lake everyone had fun swimming and diving. Then they sat by the lake and ate their supper. Things tasted so good!

After supper Beth and Dom were resting. Red began to play his fiddle. Bill and Manny were hunting for things on the beach, and Kathy was biting into the last cooky.

Just then Kathy began to cry. "Why are

you crying, Kathy?" asked her dad. "We were all joking and having fun just a second ago. What's the matter?"

But Kathy kept on crying. Her mother went to her and said, "Don't cry, honey. Tell me why you're crying."

Then Red began to do some funny tricks for Kathy. She stopped crying.

"Look, Mom and Dad," said Kathy. "When I bit into that cooky I broke my tooth! That's what made me cry!"

"Let me see," said her mother. "Kathy, your tooth isn't broken. No, indeed! It's just time for you to get your second teeth."

"Oh, neat!" said Kathy. "I was afraid I had broken a tooth." She began poking at her tooth.

Then she said, "Look, Mom and Dad! My tooth is wiggling!" Then she took a big bite from her cooky. Just one bite, but that was the end of her tooth. It fell into her lap.

When they got home, Red gave Kathy a little glass bottle for her tooth. Kathy set the bottle on a shelf. "That's my picnic tooth," she said to herself.

Red's Song

Picnics are made for a day like today.
It's so good to spend time in the sun.
As the kids play at sliding
And seeking and hiding,
My fiddle and I have some fun.

Playing is why I like picnics so much.
All the sliding and diving's a treat.
With the sun and the sand
And the lake—it's so grand
That I don't want to stop just to eat!

keeping   seating

peeping   eating

feeding   reading

speeding   leading

bleeding

               leaning

steering

cheering   leaping

(race)   (women)   (turned)

feed	keep	steer	reading
feeding	keeping	steering	leading
speeding	peeping	cheering	bleeding

A Bike Race

Dan and Jan turned on the TV one morning. They were looking at a race. Men and women on trail bikes were speeding along big trails.

"I think I would be afraid to go that fast," said Dan.

"So would I," said Jan. "Those helmets help them stay safe. But it would still scare me."

Just then on the TV a man on a red trail bike began steering his bike into a bend. Suddenly his bike slid by the stands where all the fans were sitting. The driver was leaning and fell from his bike into the mud. When he looked up, all the other bikes were speeding along the trail. His bike had slid back onto the trail.

The driver could see three bikes speeding

along, coming at his bike. If they hit his bike, they could all crash! The fans were screaming and cheering for the other drivers.

The driver was bleeding from a big gash in his leg. But still he jumped to his feet. He dashed onto the track, grabbed his bike, and dragged it to safety. The other bikes went speeding by, just missing him!

"Wow!" said Jan. "I was afraid there was going to be a bad crash!"

"He really had to be brave to run onto the track like that," said Dan. "He saved the other drivers from a bad crash!"

A woman on a green trail bike was leading the race. She was zipping along to the finish line. Her fans were leaping to their feet, screaming, and cheering. She was keeping her lead by just a little. Then just as she got to the finish line, another driver went speeding by! There would have to be a runoff!

"That turned into quite a race!" said Jan.

"I'll say!" said Dan as he turned off the TV. "You can never tell what may happen! I would like to go to one of those someday."

Later when they were eating lunch, Jan spoke to her mom and dad. "Could we go to a trail bike race someday?"

"Tickets for seating at those races are not cheap, Jan," said Mom. "But some are cheaper than others. I'll look for ads when I'm reading."

"OK, I will, too," said Dan.

"You must be good about feeding Rags and Nat every day," said Mom. "Then we'll see about getting the tickets as a treat."

One day shortly after that, Mom came home with a big grin. When they were eating supper, she kept peeking at her handbag.

"What's up, Mom?" said Dan. "You keep grinning and peeping into your handbag."

"Well, I wasn't going to tell you yet," she said. "But I'm no good at keeping things from you. I got five tickets for the trail bike races at Queen's Glen next Sunday."

"Neat!" said Dan. "I can't wait!"

"Oh, thanks, Mom!" said Jan. "But wait a second. Why did you get five tickets?"

"Well, I spoke to Mrs. Benton. Jim is still away with his grandfather. I was thinking Kim could go to the races with us. She could really use a little treat after Jim got to go on that trip."

"Yes," said Dan, "may I go tell her about the races?"

"OK," said Mom. "Then bring her back here, and we can make our plans."

diner   piled

             smiled

baker

             striped

taped

saved

waved

bake	wave	pipe	dinner
baker	waved	stripe	diner
baked	saved	striped	

Lunch at a Diner

On Sunday morning the Bells piled into the van. "We will stop for Kim and then be on our way," said Dad. "It's quite a drive to Queen's Glen, so we will want to eat before we get there. Can you think of a spot to eat, Dot?"

"There's a little diner by Twin Springs that has a good baker and cook. I taped the address in my book. How about eating there, Tom? We can get a good meal," said Mom.

"That's fine with me," said Dad. "How about you kids?"

"That's OK, Dad," said Dan and Jan.

When they got to the Bentons' house, Kim hopped into the van and waved good-by. "I'm so glad you asked me to go with you," she said. "I really like trail bike races."

"Well, we're on our way," said Mom. It was quite a drive to Queen's Glen, but the sun was shining. It was a fine day.

When they got to Twin Springs, they stopped at the little diner. A man in a striped jacket told them to sit in a big booth near a window. "Thank you," said Jan.

In a little bit, he came back. "May I take your order now?" he asked.

They all told him what they wanted to eat. He smiled and said, "I'll get this as quickly as I can." In just seconds he was back with their meals. "I hope you enjoy your meals," he said.

When they had nearly finished, he came back to their booth. "Our baker just baked some date-nut cakes and some lemon cakes," he said. "They are fresh and quite good. Would you like some?" he added.

Dad, Jan, Kim, and Dan had lemon cake. Mom saved her date-nut cake for later.

When they had finished, the waiter cleared away their plates. "I hope all of you enjoyed your meal," he said.

"Very much," said Mom.

After they had paid their bill, they got back into the van. Jan said, "Well, if the races are as good as the meal, it will be a very good day!"

At the Races

After lunch Dan, Jan, Kim, and Mr. and Mrs. Bell piled into the van and were on their way. They sang to pass the time as they went along. In just a short time they were at Queen's Glen and running to the gate. After handing in their tickets, they looked for their seats. They were quite happy with them when they got there.

"I can see everything from here!" said Dan.

"These are good seats, Dot," said Mr. Bell. "I'm glad we came."

"So am I," said Mrs. Bell.

Just seconds later, the bikes were coming onto the track. There were ten bikes in all. They lined up one by one. The fans stood up, eager to see the race begin. A flag flashed, and the bikes were off!

The fans screamed and cheered! The drivers zipped along the tracks, leaning into the bends and speeding past the stands. They seemed to go faster and faster each time they passed the stands.

"This is the last lap!" Jan said to Kim. "It's going to be a close race, just like the one on TV!"

Then a driver in a red jacket sped across the finish line. A man flashed a checkered flag. It was just a split second before the next bike crossed the line.

"What a race!" said Kim. "And there are more races to come! Oh, thank you for bringing me. This is going to be such a good day!"

far

car

jar

star

card

hard

◯ water   ◯ wash

jar	care	fair	yard
bar	car	fare	hard
star	card	far	card

A Way To Make Money

It was a hot sunny day in June. Some of the children on Grove Street sat on Pam Sands's back porch. They were trying to think of a way to make money. They wanted to go to the zoo that week, but it was so far they had to go by bus. They needed money for the fare.

"I can drive you in the car if you want me to," said Mr. Sands, Pam's dad.

"Thanks, Dad," said Pam. "But this time we would like to go alone. We can take the bus, if that's OK with you."

"That's fine, honey," said Mr. Sands as he went back into the house.

"I need a drink," said Pam. "Who wants a glass of water?"

"I do," said Sam. "I wanted a drink of

water a long time ago, but our kitchen was being mopped."

So Pam went inside and got glasses of water for all of them. When she came back to the porch, she nearly dropped her tray. "I've got it!" she said. "That's how we can make money!"

"What? What's it?" said Linda. "How can we make the money?"

"We can wash cars!" said Pam. "Lots of drivers would like to have their cars washed, and hundreds of cars pass by on Grove Street. The drivers will be happy to stop and let us wash the mud from their cars!"

"That's good thinking, Pam," said Sam. "When can we have this car wash?"

"Well, we'd better do it today," said Pam. "We need the money by Sunday."

"OK," said Sam. "I can get some big planks of wood and some nails. We can set up a stand to collect our money."

"I can get a hose and a pan for the suds. We'll need lots and lots of suds," said Pam.

"Good," said Linda. "I can get some rags. That should do it."

So they set up the stand. Sam nailed a big card on it. On the card they painted green stars. This is what the card said:

Grove Street Car Wash

Help us get to the zoo.

Pam got a jar from the kitchen to keep the money in. The children didn't wash a single car that day. A team of men and women came to patch the potholes on Grove Street with tar. So no cars passed their stand all day.

The next day Pam and Linda made little cards that told about the car wash. They took the cards to the houses on Grove Street. They had some cards left, so they went to the houses on Eleventh Street, too.

After a long time, the tar was dry. Cars began to pass the stand. A red car stopped, and Linda yelled, "We'll wash your car for a dollar!"

The driver of the car said, "Is Sixth Street far from here?"

"Not far," said Pam. "Would you like us to wash your car for a dollar?"

"I don't think so, thank you," said the driver. Then she drove off.

By this time Pam, Linda, and Sam were

beginning to think they had picked a hard way to get money. They sat on the steps to think. A woman went by in a very muddy car. "That car really needs to be washed," said Sam. "I'll ask her."

"Would you like us to wash your car for a dollar?" Sam asked.

"Why, yes," said the woman. She parked her car in Pam's driveway. When they had finished washing her car, the woman gave Pam a five-dollar bill. But they had no single dollars to give back to the woman.

Pam gave the five-dollar bill back to the woman. Then Pam said, "That car wash was free. Thank you for stopping."

So the children had to close the car wash. Mr. Sands didn't really want them to go that far alone, so he was glad to drive them.

bark   cart

dark   part

lark   start

farm

farmer

alarm

arm

bird

star	far	bar	car
start	farm	bark	cart
part	farmer	lark	card

The Zoo

That Sunday was a fine sunny day. Gus, Linda, Pam, and Sam got into the van and started for the zoo.

Gus said to Pam, "I'm glad to drive you to the zoo. I enjoy seeing all the animals, too."

"I'm glad you came with us," said Pam.

It was a short trip in the van. They got there in no time at all. Gus parked the van by a dark green pine tree. It was quite a hike from the parking lot to the gate. The zoo had little carts that ran from the parking lots to the gate.

"Are these cart rides free?" asked Gus as they hopped on.

"Yes, they are," said the driver. "There are

carts inside that cost money. If you wish, you can ride them to different parts of the zoo."

"I see," said Gus. "I think we'll just use our feet and save our money."

When they had paid for their tickets, they all went inside. "What do you want to see?" said Gus.

"May we go to see the birds?" asked Linda.

"OK," said Gus, Pam, and Sam. There were lots and lots of birds. They looked at cardinals, hummingbirds, woodpeckers, larks, and peacocks.

Then Pam wanted to go to the part of the zoo where the snakes were kept. But Sam didn't want to go.

Gus patted him on the arm and said, "Don't let them alarm you. All the snakes are in glass tanks. They are all closed in, so it's quite safe."

"Well, OK," said Sam. But he still wasn't very happy about looking at snakes.

After they had looked at all the snakes, they went to the part of the zoo that had farm animals. "I like this part best," said Sam. "I like cows, horses, and hogs better than snakes. Maybe I'll be a farmer someday."

"I think that's a smart thing to do," said Gus.

Then Sam added, "And I'll get a dog that barks to keep the snakes away!"

A Map of the Zoo

This map tells where all the different animals are in the zoo. Can you tell where Gus, Linda, Pam, and Sam went?

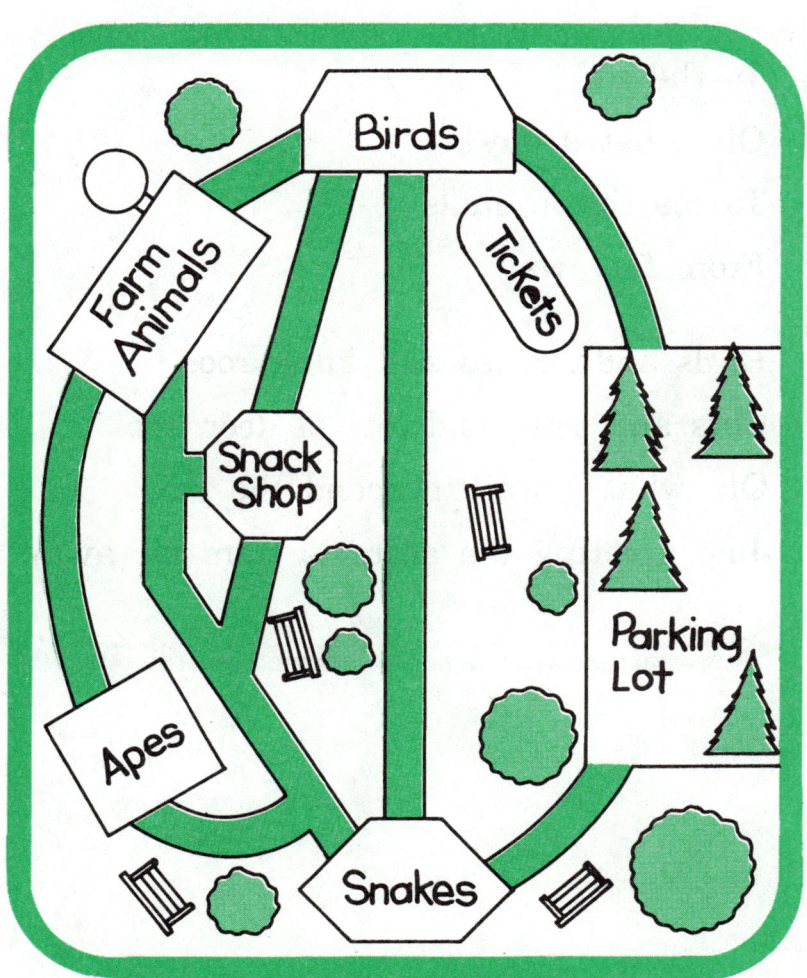

To the Zoo

To the zoo. To the zoo.
Oh, what a day!
To see the animals
From far away.

Birds and snakes and kangaroos,
Cats and cows and lots of deer, too.
Oh, what a way to spend the day,
Just greeting the animals from far away.

tall

ball

call

fall

small

all	tale	fair	smart
ball	tall	fail	small
small	call	fall	

One Inch Taller

Nick was small, and not very tall. No one seemed to care about his size. But Nick cared. He didn't like being smaller than the rest of the boys. He wished he could be just one inch taller.

In September when school had started, Nick had taped a strip on his wall. Whenever he reached that mark, he would be one inch taller. Now it was June, the last day of school, and Nick still had not reached the mark. "Just about," he kept saying to himself. "I'm just about there." And every day he would be just about there, but not quite—not yet.

One summer day Nick was playing ball with Frank and Cal. "Let's do something different," Nick said.

"I've got it!" said Cal. "We can fill this box with rocks and pretend it's a chest of gold."

"Then we can hide it in the woods," Frank added.

Then Nick said, "OK, let's do it. It'll be fun, but we'll need to pack a lunch."

So they went home to pack the lunch. Nick made a peanut butter and jelly sandwich and filled a jar with milk. He shut the lunch in his backpack and fastened the pack on his back.

"Someone's going to have a real feast," Nick's mother said to him. "Well, have a good trip, and be back by six."

The boys met Cal at her house. "Let me call Muff," Cal said. "She's asleep in the hall." Then she called, "Come on, Muff. Let's get started on our little trip."

"Wake up, Muff," yelled Frank and Nick, "or you'll miss all the fun!"

At last Cal's fat cat woke up. Then they all started for the woods. They pretended a big log was the ship. "Sit still, Muff, or you may fall into the water," Cal said. "This is a big river we have to cross."

They pretended to sail for a long time. At last they got across the water. They sat under a big tree to eat their lunches. When they had finished, Frank said, "Let's hide our chest of gold."

But Nick just sat there. "I think I'll stay here for a bit," he said. "I ate too much."

So Frank and Cal picked up the chest. "Come on, Muff," they called, and off they went.

As Nick lay resting under the tree, he

looked up. How very tall the tree was! It seemed to reach the sky. "I wish I could be as tall as this tree," Nick said to himself. Then he said, "Well, maybe not that tall!"

Suddenly someone was calling, "Nick, you'll have to come help us!" It was Cal and Frank.

"What's the problem?" Nick asked as they came up to him.

"Something scared Muff," Frank said, "and she ran up a tree. She's up there now, and we can't get her to jump."

When they got back to the spot where they had left her, Muff was crying. "She's really scared up there," Cal said.

"Wait," said Nick. "I have a plan that cannot fail." Then he dumped his milk jar from his pack and started up the tree with the empty pack on his arm. Inch by inch, Nick wiggled up the trunk. Then branch by branch, up and up he went until he could reach the cat. He stuck Muff into his pack and twisted the pack onto his back. Then he took Muff safely to the bottom of the tree. Frank and Cal were cheering and clapping and yelling, "You saved her! You saved Muff!"

At last they collected their things to go home. This time they didn't ride on their ship. When they got to Nick's house, Cal and Frank told Nick's mother all about Nick's brave deed. His mother was so happy she smiled and gave her son a big, big hug. "You're a real hero, Nick," she said.

Nick puffed up his chest. Had he just gotten taller? Well, he really felt he had, and that was the best feeling of all.

TO THE TEACHER

The MERRILL READING PROGRAM consists of eight Readers developed on linguistic principles applicable to the teaching of reading. The rationale of the program and detailed teaching procedures are described in the Teacher's Edition of each Reader.

All words introduced in this Reader are listed on the following pages under the headings "Words in Pattern," "Sight Words," and "Applications of Patterning."

Words listed as "Words in Pattern" represent matrices in the second and third major sets of spelling patterns. Words in the second major set differ from those in the first set by the addition of the letter e at the end. Words in the third major set are characterized by vowel combinations before final consonants or consonant combinations. In addition, some pattern pages present pattern words with the endings -*ing*, -*er*, and -*ed*. Two minor sets of spelling patterns are presented at the end of the Reader. These sets contain the vowel-consonant combinations *ar* and *all*.

Words listed as "Sight Words" are high-frequency words introduced to provide normal sentence patterns in the stories.

Words listed as "Applications of Patterning" include new words based on patterns and sight words previously introduced, combinations of words (compound words), additional tense forms, plurals, possessives, and contractions.

WORD LISTS FOR TEACHER REFERENCE

Pages	Words in Pattern	Sight Words	Pages	Words in Pattern	Sight Words
Unit 1 5-10	cape tape cane Jane	which across	Unit 6 35-40	hope note rode drove joke broke broken bone alone	their
Unit 2 11-16	ate came same tame name game	son			
Unit 3 17-22	hide ride side ripe pipe		Unit 7 41-46	use cute cube tube tune	zoo
Unit 4 23-28	pale paste taste waste gave brave		Unit 8 47-52	bake lake Jake safe five live drive alive	
Unit 5 29-34	slide stripe quite life wife		Unit 9 53-58	hose rose those these	

Pages	Words in Pattern	Sight Words	Pages	Words in Pattern	Sight Words
Unit 10 59-64	sail tail pail mail Gail waist		Unit 13 77-82 cont.	tree three steer queer seem seen teens	
Unit 11 65-70	paid laid rain pain paint plain fair pair hair wait		Unit 14 83-88	meat beat eat treat sea tea read real heal dear hear	
Unit 12 71-76	feed need meet feet feel heel deep keep sheep creep steep		Unit 15 89-94	weak beak speak peach teach each leaf least beast east cheap	does
Unit 13 77-82	week seek peek sweet street				

Pages	Words in Pattern	Sight Words	Pages	Words in Pattern	Sight Words
Unit 16 95-100	taping baking taking making shaking hoping using		Unit 19 113-118	diner baker taped saved waved piled smiled striped	
Unit 17 101-106	hiking hiding riding sliding diving driving biting poking joking	too tooth	Unit 20 119-124	far car jar star card hard	water wash
Unit 18 107-112	keeping peeping feeding speeding bleeding steering cheering seating eating reading leading leaning leaping	race women turned	Unit 21 125-130	bark dark lark farm farmer alarm arm cart part start	bird
			Unit 22 131-137	tall ball call fall small	

Applications of Patterning
(The underlined numbers are page numbers.)

Unit 1 5-10	Unit 3 17-22 cont.	Unit 5 29-34	Unit 6 35-40 cont.
Banks	giggle	different	ketchup
beginning	hospital	dressing	lumpy
boss	Hunter's	dumped	mustard
bumped	inside	enter	napkins
couldn't	magnet	grant	packets
everything	magnets	grin	picnic
flowers	opened	helpers	plastic
Franklin	others	husband	risk
more	pipes	littering	short
open	pocket	lunches	sons
pretend	snake	old	tonsils
rushing	snakes	quit	visited
tapped	swimming	second	

Unit 2 11-16	tricks underside understood wiggle	seconds strip stripes suppers	Unit 7 41-46
boy's		torn	ape
camping	Unit 4 23-28	unless	apes
fingers		walls	benches
forever			classes
fresh	blame		collected
games	cabinets		cubes
Hunter	clinic	Unit 6 35-40	everyone
lad	fine		fins
mushrooms	flinch		flamingo
played	grade	backed	gate
seven	grinned	bananas	gray
shelf	happen	bones	late
Specks'	Long's	boys'	later
Tammy	mending	camped	morning
thinks	mixer	checkup	ostrich
understand	mixing	checkups	ostriches
won't	ones	dump	otters
Unit 3 17-22	puppet rubber running shouldn't	family finish grill happened	pay planned riddles save
clapped	sides	Hicks	splashed
clips	stacking	infected	stayed
drifted	stitched	jokes	
Ed's	stuff		
Freddy	telling		

Applications of Patterning
(The underlined numbers are page numbers.)

Unit 7　41-46 cont.	Unit 8　47-52 cont.	Unit 10　59-64 cont.	Unit 11　65-70 cont.
strong	shatter	dogs'	fare
tasted	shifted	drag	Fathers
together	shine	eleven	fifth
tubes	snake's	finished	grabbed
tunes	spoke	flash	handbag
used	tack	Gail's	handles
won't	they'll	Hank	huffing
wouldn't	understanding	Hank's	Kent
	wiggled	having	line
	wiggling	Jill	longer
Unit 8　47-52		Jill's	Monday
		Kelly	Mothers
		letters	plane
asking	**Unit 9　53-58**	mailbox	puffing
backbone		pig's	rains
belongs		plenty	sailors
Betty	glory	quick	state
blacksnake	interest	sails	takes
blacksnakes	Mother's	sale	terminal
bookshelf	popped	Sally	ticket
born	protect	sudden	tickets
cutting	roses	tails	waiting
dropped	select	tale	woke
fangs	silly	wipe	
hatched	smell		
helpful	sniff		
insects	spray		
Jones	spraying		
lesson	thorns	**Unit 11　65-70**	**Unit 12　71-76**
lessons	upon		
nine		afraid	beet
person		airplane	dentist
pests		airport	flock
racks	**Unit 10　59-64**	begins	lame
rake		besides	mustn't
rattlesnakes		Bond	nibbling
ribs	bite	Bonds	named
rust	cake	classrooms	Nan
schools	candles	clipped	Peggy
shade	crying		

Applications of Patterning
(The underlined numbers are page numbers.)

Unit 12 71-76 cont.	Unit 13 77-82 cont.	Unit 15 89-94	Unit 16 95-100 cont.
pep	sixteen	airline	crutch
sleep	smile	airlines	Dom
struck	someone	bare	Don
tend	tricked	beach	dusting
tending	weeks	care	enjoy
thorn		cheaper	gash
		doesn't	grinning
		dresser	hopping
		grandson	hundred
		hotel	lately
		June	offer
Unit 13 77-82	Unit 14 83-88	leak	pained
		meeting	press
	add	nearby	Red's
bands	being	needs	Santis
bee	bookshop	packing	sitter's
beside	clams	pile	stronger
bitter	dime	quickly	taken
Bob	feelers	rates	unbend
brings	hobby	reached	whatever
buzz	interesting	scrape	
Candy	jellyfish	shame	
children's	lobster	shorts	
Deb	lobsters	skipper	Unit 17 101-106
drummer	neat	snapshots	
drummers	really	stays	
drumsticks	reeds	stepped	bottle
fifteen	sailor	teacher	cooky
flute	seaweed	tenth	diving's
Fran	shellfish		fiddle
Main	shops		grand
Nell	shrimp		hike
nineteen	skiff	Unit 16 95-100	honey
nodded	skins		hunting
pals	sort		indeed
pucker	teacup	backing	Kathy
Ron	themselves	badly	matter
seemed	visiting	Beth	peaches
sister	whenever	cross	picnics

Applications of Patterning

(The underlined numbers are page numbers.)

Unit 17 101-106 cont.	Unit 19 113-118	Unit 20 119-124	Unit 21 125-130	Unit 22 131-137 cont.
sandwich	added	bar	barks	deed
sandwiches	baked	cards	birds	empty
seeking	bends	cars	cardinals	fail
stairs	booth	carts	carts	fastened
teeth	bringing	collect	closed	feast
wink	cakes	dollar	cost	feeling
	checkered	dollars	cows	gold
	cheered	driveway	greeting	gotten
Unit 18 107-112	cleared	eleventh	hummingbirds	hall
	close	free	kangaroos	hero
	crossed	glasses	larks	it'll
ads	date	Grove	parking	jelly
coming	eager	houses	parts	lay
dashed	enjoyed	hundreds	peacocks	mark
driver	flashed	nailed	pine	Muff
drivers	handing	nails	rides	Nick's
Glen	lemon	needed	seeing	peanut
green	meal	painted	smart	pretended
helmets	meals	parked	started	problem
peeking	near	planks	woodpeckers	puffed
Queen's	nearly	porch		reach
races	order	potholes	Unit 22 131-137	river
runoff	plates	Sands's		safely
safety	screamed	single		scared
scare	seats	stars		size
screaming	shining	tar	asleep	smaller
shortly	sped	team	branch	someone's
stands	split	washed	butter	taller
suddenly	Springs	washing	Cal	wake
trail	waiter	yard	called	wall
trails	wave		calling	wished
what's			Cal's	yelling
zipping			cared	
			clapping	